Ray L. Birdwhistell
Dept. of Psychology and Social Anthropology
University of Louisville

INTRODUCTION TO KINESICS:

(An annotation system for analysis of body motion and gesture)

c

UNIVERSITY OF LOUISVILLE

LOUISVILLE 8, KENTUCKY

p.3, numbered paragraph 2, end of parenthesis: insert p. no.-35.

p.5, 3rd line of text: willingness <u>on</u> the part....

p.26,
> Item 1. - Insert ⌒ after ‖ over Mama.
> 6. - Change "whisper" to "openness."
>
> 8. - The symbol for rasp is ⸮ , not "?".

p.29,
> Item 2. - Insert ⌒ after ‖ before ³ calls ²| ⌒ .
> 3. - Delete ⌒ after People, and insert ⌒ before ³ over dying. Delete ＼ over -ing and over to. Insert ⌃ at beginning of second line, before meet. Change ∧ to ／ over meet. Insert ⋀ under ⌒ after meet. Change／ to ＼ over you. Delete ³ before you, and ⌒ after you. Insert ＼ after all ⌒ . Place ⌃／⌃ over -bout. Delete ³ before you, change ⌒／ to ＼ over you, delete ⌒ after you.
> 4. - Insert ／ at end of first line.

p.31-2,
> Item 1. - Delete ＼ over second syllable of Hiyah. Do the same in items 2, 6, 7.
> 2. - Delete ² over -cha. Change ∧ to ／ over doing. —Delete ∪ over - cha and wherever else it occurs. ?
> 3. - Change ＼ to ／ over Pig- and delete ／ over -gin. Delete ³ between cha and doing.
> 4. - Delete ¹ before and after for. Insert ¹ after guys.
> 5. - Insert ¹ after Smithers. Change ／ to ＼ over From, delete ＼ over -mond.
> 8. - Delete ¹ and ∧ over ya. Insert ¹ after in.
> 9. - Insert ³ after First before ＼ .
> 11. - Change ∧ to ＼ over I. Delete ∧ over was.

TABLE OF CONTENTS

PREFACE

This paper represents an attempt to outline certain aspects of the study of body motion and communication for the use of students and researchers in this field. It is intended as an introduction to, rather than as a definitive summary or review of, research in the field of body motion and meaning.

Section I consists of a brief discussion of the general field of kinesics which, it is hoped, will be suggestive to others working in this area whether their central focus be linguistic, psychiatric, or general cultural. The field of kinesics is divided methodologically in a manner approximating the prevalent usage in linguistics. While I take full responsibility for any of the theoretical statements below, I must acknowledge my great debt to Drs. George L. Trager and Henry Lee Smith, Jr. The suggestions of these two linguist-anthropologists during a six month seminar on the relationship between linguistic and kinesic phenomena guided the development of much of the following discussion.

Section II presents an annotation system for the recording of body motion. Somewhat more complex than other annotational systems, it has been designed specifically for the recording and analysis of cross-cultural data. It is not complete. The total range of possible variation in muscle activity is not recorded in this limited list of symbols. It is, however, so designed that it will permit considerable expansion according to its basic logic. Further research should certainly lead to its revision.

Introduction to Kinesics is a preliminary research manual. It has been developed and is presented with the hope that it will stimulate research in this almost-neglected area of human interaction. The paper is the result of the crystallization and integration of the author's researches taking place during his stay at the Foreign Service Institute in the Spring of 1952 as Visiting Lecturer in Psychology. Acknowledgment is gratefully made for the opportunity thus offered to present these materials.

Ray L. Birdwhistell

Washington, D. C.
May 15, 1952.

2.

Section I: A PRELIMINARY REVIEW

The following represents an attempt to review certain methodological aspects of the study of body motion as related to the non-verbal aspects of inter-personal communication. The term kinesics has been chosen to cover the multi-level approach (physical, physiological, psychological, and cultural) to such phenomena. To minimize the conceptual differences between the various social sciences the term social kinesiologist has been selected as the term for one attempting to analyze systematically the data covered by kinesic investigation.

. The discussion will fall unequally into four major categories. To clarify the writer's position, certain primary conceptions which at present govern the field of kinesics will introduce this section. Following this,.the field of kinesics will be outlined.

The study of kinesics may be divided into three major categories:

1. Pre-kinesics, which deals with general physiological bases for the systematic study of body-motion.

2. Micro-kinesics, which deals with the isolation of kines (least particles of abstractable body motion - see Section II, p.35) which aims at the abstraction of kines into manageable morphological classes.

3. Social kinesics, which relates to the functioning of motion as related to social performance. Social performance here relates to/the communication aspects of social interaction whether such behavior involves integrational or new informational performance.

The use of "integrational" as opposed to "new informational" may prove artificial but, for the time being, these categories may be distinguished. "Integrational" communication involves such interaction as.invokes common past experience

and is related to the initiation, maintenance,
or severance of interaction. "New informational", while symbolically consistent with and
made up of past experience, involves the inclu-
sion of information not held in common by the
communicants.

The aims of this paper are such that the discussion below
is general and makes no specific reference to documentary material on body motion. The reader will find a partial bibliography
at the end of the paper. As stated in the preface, this is intended as a suggestive report rather than a definitive coverage
of the metaphysical or physiological bases for motion research.

1. Preconceptions of Kinesics.

Primary to any systematic examination of such phenomena as that represented by the movements of the human body in its higher level activities as a member unit in the cultural context is the willingness on the part of the investigator to relinquish assumptions which relate to "accidental" or "meaningless" activity. Once taken, this step eradicates the vitiating inclination to dump non-traceable activities into either the "independent particle" or the "idiosyncratic" wastebasket. Thus, any movement from a heuristic zero point in space-time represents a bit of behavior subject to analysis.

It is recognized that both temperamental and cultural differences will effect the "zero point." Thus, as translated for middle class Americans the zero point, repose, is assumed as the "semi-relaxed" state of the body. All zero points must be defined with cultural-indicating prefixes. On the living body, any perceptible position is a motion from zero.

Social personality is a tempero-spacial system. All behaviors evinced by any such system are components of the system except as related to differential levels of abstractions. "A" behavior and "the" system or field of force are inseparable. Thus, research may reveal any given particle of motion to be more or less important as measured against a given problem, but no particle can occupy a position independent from the field of force.

Even if no participant of an interaction field can recall, or repeat in a dramatized context, a given series or sequence of motions, the appearance of a motion is of significance to the general study of the particular kinesic system even if the given problem can be rationalized without reference to it.

"Dramatized context" as used hereafter will refer to a repetition of a kinesic act or action pattern in the informant-investigation situation. Context as used will refer to any observed kinesic pattern in which the observer does not direct the action.

6.

Thus, any given motion may have relative insignificance on one level of generalization or problem but may be of the greatest significance on another.

> E.g., the medial brow pinch or mid-face frown may be related to vocalization as (a) an allo-kine (or equivalent meaning particle) of an intonation marking nod; (b) as an indication socially either of annoyance or attention; (c) may be idiokinesically defined as a repose station.

While every attempt should be made to isolate and make recordable the possible variations of motion, only continuing systematization of motion patterns will provide silhouettes against which the importance of variation can be measured.

> Gestalt and field theory will probably dominate kinesic analysis. However, kines must be recorded for idiokinesic and diakinesic analysis. Kinesic analysis must depend on sufficient evidence concerning general patterning.

A second major point underlying the field of kinesics relates to the proposition that all meaningful motion patterns are to be regarded as socially learned until empirical investigation reveals otherwise.

It has been generally agreed that "gestures", i.e., conventionalized motor symbols, are learned. (I say "generally agreed", for there are scholars who would assign many of these to some kind of universal symbolism which emerge from "basic needs.") That there is an infinite number of other motor patterns which are socially learned and have social meaning is not so generally accepted. A few of these are regarded as "expressive gestures" and as relatable only to the experience of the particular individuals; most are simply ignored or assumed to be "natural." It is the experience of the research upon which this paper is based that such a priori judgments are often fallacious.

As an example, we may take a pattern like the eye-lids. Even in the face of such culturally revealing statements as "She batted her eyes at him," variations in lid behavior are often dismissed as "accidental" or described in a reductionist manner which relates to the "primary" functioning of the eye as an aid to ball lubrication or as shields against intense light frequencies or intrusive particles.

It is evident that the range of learning possible in the lid complex is considerable. Examination of cases provided by South Asian religious cults makes this clear. A fakir can, after intensive training, inhibit the lid in the full glare of the sun or while the ball is being peltered by dust-laden air.

Preliminary investigation of the relationship between body motion and verbal behavior indicates that lid activity may be closely correlated with such finite patterning of speech behavior as stress, voice qualifiers, and intonation patterns. There is considerable evidence that as such linguistic behavior varies from culture to culture so does the accompanying supportive (?) or definitive lid behavior.

> I am not suggesting a necessary correlation of particular lid behaviors with particular stress, voice qualifiers, or intonation systems in any extra-cultural fashion. The observation of bilingual speakers indicate that these are semi-independent systems which must be examined in context. The significant aspect of this is that as a bilingual speaker changes languages he also changes kinesic systems. As will be stressed later, there seems to be no more universality to the meaning of kinesic patterns than there is to any sound pattern.

Some authors make a differentiation between "learning" and "maturation." To them "learning" covers those shifts in behavior which are derived from experience. The assumption in this review that motion patterns are socially learned does not indicate a lack of sympathy with such a distinction. Nor does this contradict the findings of such studies as those being carried on by Gesell and his students. Recent studies of this school have indicated that the rate of development of given children may be effected by their particular social milieus. This, taken together with the insights given by Mead in her study of Balinese children, would suggest that considerable caution must be exerted in making statements which assign a discretely biological base to given motions.

It is hoped that kinesics will not become lost in a nature-nurture argument. If the pre-kinesic analysis is rigorously done there need be no such dichotomy set up. However, since we are primarily concerned with the communication aspects of body motion, and since communication patterns seem to be learned phenomena, all particles will be treated as learned until universals are shown from cross-cultural research. This point is stressed because the ethnocentric definition of "natural" may provide burial grounds for important and revealing research.

As related to the analysis of social kinesics or "expressive" behavior, I am tentatively adopting a "whole body" conception. Portions of such activity may be beyond thresholds of sensory perception. Their presence may only have been determined by the use of sensory multipliers such as galvanometers, electro-encephalographs, sphygmomanometers, etc.. However, outside of such data, which lie beyond the range of the unassisted senses, there exists a significant amount of "private" behavior which can be isolated by the trained kinesics observer without recourse to these paraphanalia.

In fact, kinesiologists may discover, as have linguists, that not only do such complicated recording devices impose certain limitations upon the research situation, but they often provide non-significant data (that is, non-significant to the problems being analyzed by the student of human communication). The acoustician records data imperceptible to even the most trained observer. Such events are of little interest to the student of vocal communication except insofar as they aid in his analysis of the raw data. Similarly, such machines as the sphygmomanometer may give support to the conclusions of the social kinesiologist but are not substitutes for the trained human observer. (This extends to the use of moving pictures). If phenomena cannot be observed through the unassisted senses (of the "normal" observer), such phenomena are of little significance to participants in interaction, except as related to introspective pick-up which may influence the actor's behavioral series.

> An example of the above might be the situation in which the young girl changes stance and exhibits "restless" behavior when a breeze ruffles a look of her hair. Obviously, she is "picking up" a follicular response which may be quite imperceptible to the "outside" observer. One might suggest that the stimulus is unimportant and that the fact that the restless behavior appears is the important aspect of this situation. Until such behavior is examined in a series of contrasting contexts no final analytic description can be made.

Related to the above discussion, a few remarks must be directed to the problem of "recall", "informants' descriptions", and "conscious-unconscious" dichotomies. (I am deeply grateful to Smith and Trager for sensitizing me to this in relation to work with linguistic informants.) . For the time being I shall use two concepts which are designed to cover the difference between that behavior which may be recalled by the informant-actor and repeated upon request, and that which cannot be recalled and which may even be denied by the actor. For the first of these the term indicative will be used; for the second, the term expressive has been applied.

I must stress the fact that the differences between these two kinds of behavior are probably limited. The fact that a given informant can repeat upon request, a particular motion may not, for certain problems, be significantly different from a motion which the informant cannot recall.

For instance, there may appear a pattern in which the nostrils are pinched between the thumb and forefinger with fingers 3, 4 and 5 remaining lax and with the brows bi-laterally and minimally raised. The informant will be able to state that this symbolizes the occurrence of an event, chemically unrelated to an odor-carrying gas, which "stinks". Under analysis, this may not differ from the "involuntary" soft passage of these same fingers near the nose in a minimally produced "nose holding", and which the informant cannot recall. The contextual difference must be discovered before the acts can be described as having differential social meaning. On certain levels of analysis these acts are the same, on others, they will differ considerably. However, the "gesture" is not a "stronger", or a "truer" representation per se of attitude than is the non-recallable act.

Neither the nose-holding (impolite or extravagant usage) American nor, for comparison, the ear-pinching Portugese (signalling passage of an attractive female) is necessarily conscious of the broader cultural orientations of which their gestures may be representations. Behind the American's gesture lies a configuration of training and experience which symbolically relates "bad" and negative olfactory sensations. Behind the Portugese ear pull is a configuration of culture which emphasizes considerable verbalization of the delights of the relations between the sexes.

Anthropologists who have attempted to use conceptions such as "covert" and "overt", "explicit" and "implicit" (useful as teaching devices) in their empirical research know the pitfalls of such devices. Particularly at this stage of the research in body motion as related to meaning, the researcher must be very careful not to reify the conscious vs. the unconscious "mind". "Breadth" of meaning should reflect carefully organized and stated problems rather than preconceptions idealistically and duallistically formed. From this point of view we may generalize that an informant's statement concerning the "meaning" of his particular act (or lack of such a statement) is behavior which accompanies the act and should not be given weighted value in its interpretation.

Summary

A. No motion is a thing in itself. It is always a part of a pattern. There is no "meaningless" motor activity.

B. Until otherwise demonstrated, body motion patterns should be regarded as socially learned.

C. No unit of motion carries meaning per se. Meaning arises in context.

D. An informant's statement regarding his own motion should be regarded as data rather than explanation.

2. Prekinesics.

It is probably possible to study social kinesic phenomena without recourse to physiological data, just as it is
possible to study literature without understanding the voice
box and its place in the physiological system. If, however,
we regard the problems confronting the kinesiologist as more
nearly comparable to those of the linguist, it is evident
that our generalizations concerning any particular motion or
motion pattern is sound only if we can control the physiological aspects of our problems.

Notwithstanding the statement that motion patterning is
to be regarded as socially learned, the fact remains that
every motion involves the physiological system. Intensity,
frequency, and even choice of certain motions are limited by
and may even be determined by the state of the physiological
system. The variations provided by physiological differenti-
ations are obviously of little concern if the problem involved
in the examination of the data is culturological. On the
other hand, any attempt to analyze the motion system of a
particular individual must involve understanding of the particular physiological state.

The kinesiologist should be equipped to at least read the
material concerning the relationships between the neurological,
the endocrinological, and kinesthesiological systems. He
should have a working knowledge of the kinesthesiological system
and its relationship with the skeletal structure. All of this
will aid in his observation and description of body activities.

In the social sciences, few workers are able to maintain
pace with their own and parallel fields and at the same time
keep up with the material accumulating from the physical and
biological sciences. It seems likely that much of the intensive work done in the area of kinesics will have to be done
by interdisciplinary teams. This lacking, the social kinesiologist should at least have access to advice from specialists
from the physical and biological sciences.

The social kinesiologist must remember that there are
only certain kinds of information which he should seek from
the physiologist, the endocrinologist, the kinesthesiologist,
or even, the psychiatrist-psychologist. These are statements

which relate to the primary foci of their varied researches.
He should be exceedingly cautious about assuming that because these experts are skilled with regard to the description of the internal relationships of the muscle-skeletal system,
or of the physiological system, or of psycho-somatically defined
phenomena, that they are necessarily expert in the area of body
motion and meaning, particularly as these are studied in a cross-
cultural context.

On the other hand, if the social kinesiologist's cultural
determinism prevents him from gaining the insights which may
be provided by association in the interdisciplinary situation,
his rigidity will be reflected in his work. If the research
is genuinely interdisciplinary, both the biological and the
social scientist should derive great benefit from the cross-
fertilization.

The ideal interdisciplinary situation would include all
of the specialists mentioned above. However, any realistic
appraisal of the bars to such interdisciplinary cooperation
brings the realization that, at least for the present, most
workers will not have an opportunity for such rewarding association. In most universities and hospitals (not to exclude
government-sponsored research situations) departmentaliza-
tion is sufficiently rigid to prevent the evolution of such
projects as are envisaged above. However, the skills needed
for the analysis of pre-kinesic data may be embodied in the
physiological psychologist. Indeed, his particular training
may be more adaptable to research on pre-kinesics than those
of the forementioned scientists.

A review of the literature (see Suggested Readings) reveals that the activity of the skeleto-muscular system has
concerned various psychologists over the past half-century
or more. Little of this work has much to do with the understanding of social kinesics, being either so philosophical
or strictly biological in nature as to be quite untranslatable
in communication terms.

On the other hand, there does exist a body of material
which casts light upon some of our primary problems. Of particular importance is that work which has examined the relationship between endocrine states and muscle tension and activity.
It is unfortunate, for our purposes, that so little cross-
cultural checking has been done of this kind of material.
Much of it must, as far as the social kinesiologist is concerned, remain no more than suggestive because of the ethnocentric categories which have dominated the research.

No less regrettable is the lack, in such material, of sufficiently explicit reporting of the social position, cultural identifications, or personal histories either of the subjects reported on or of the control groups utilized in the testing of the data. Much of the earlier material is frankly racist, articles published as late as 1940, using such gross categories as "Negro" for comparison purposes.

I have perhaps overstressed the difficulty of organizing interdisciplinary research on body motion. A major proportion of these difficulties derive from a failure to have sufficiently explicit categories upon which the membership of the various fields can concentrate. It is hoped that the kinegraphs presented in Section II will aid in meeting this problem. If the worker will be methodologically strict, his work will be expedited and his generalization have meaning. In this, as in the study of similar phenomena, if the levels of generalization are rigorously maintained, little difficulty of communication between fields arises.

Pre-kinesics lays the groundwork for the study of social kinesics. It should provide the worker in micro-kinesics and social kinesics with some understanding of the limits which the physiological system in its various states exerts upon performance. Lacking this information, the social kinesiologist always runs the risk of psychological or cultural determinism. With it, he has much more chance of making meaningful statements concerning either personality or social organization.

3. Microkinesics

The problem of recording and primary analysis of kinesic data has hampered research in motion since the first interest was evinced in the field of motor communication. The basic research in motion must be done before the analysis of patterning can have more than an artistic meaning. Before there can be a science of body motion there must be sufficient research done that it becomes possible to recognize the essential particles of significant patterns. Independent research may become communicable and testable by various scientists only when they are sure they are examining similar phenomena.

> I am not in such usage as this suggesting that the sciences be multiplied, I have described it thus as a device to keep this work from becoming immediately identified as a province of one or another of the traditional disciplines.

Primary to this is the necessity of deriving an orthography by means of which the particles of motion can be isolated and their pattern activity and significance empirically tested. Particularly is this necessary if we are to do cross-cultural analysis. We must have some conventionalized system of recording which can be taught to field workers and which can be independently analyzed later.

The system of annotation which is presented in section II is designed for expansion. It is admittedly clumsy, but it has shown itself useful both in direct recording and in the training of observers. The greatest objection to it, outside of its evident ethnocentrism (which can only be alleviated through extensive research and testing in various cultures), lies in the fact that it is too complex to print or handle on a typewriter. It is my hope that a simpler orthography can be improvised.

An attempt has been made to institute a different orthographic logic for each section of the body to expedite recording and later reading. The kines described below may eventually be seen to be either too gross or over-minute. Certainly, the amount of possible variation is so great that no recorder can note all parts of the body, with their respective kines,

in one observation period. It is suggested that any student
beginning kinesic recording work on but one part of the body
at a time. A fairly minute recording of one body aspect should
be taken, with mnemonic notations concerning "impressions" of
the remainder of the body. At a later session another section
of the body can be stressed. Working this way, the worker can
begin a holistic analysis of his data in a relatively short
time. As his understanding of the particular kinesic system
grows, the amount of recording will decrease. At the same time,
if the student has undergone a careful sensitization process,
his recording will become increasingly accurate and relevant.

Again the warning must be included that so little is
known at present, at least insofar as I have been able to
ascertain, about general kinesic patterning, much less diakinesic patterning, that serious errors of an autistic nature
can be made by over-easy assumption of the significance or
insignificance of particular variations.

Kinemorphs

It is evident that except for the serious student of kinesic
systems, most users of kinesic material will not be able to record and analyze every kine played by the actor in any given action
situation. This is particularly difficult for the average American mover when working with the kinesiological systems of other
Americans. It will be very difficult for the student to divorce
his own meaning-responses from the observation situation. Un-
less very carefully schooled to recognize kines other than those
which lie within his own immediate recall system, he is highly
likely either to ignore kines in the same time-action field or
fail to see them altogether. It is necessary that any user of
kinesic analysis be at least "exposed" in an introductory but
systematic fashion to the entire area of kines. It is particularly important that he be given sufficient training in the
differential systems of kines, both as seen in diakines and idio-
kines in his own culture and as expressed in the kinesic systems
of another culture so that he can gain some insight into the
problems of kinesic significances.

Not only should the student of kinesics be exposed to examples of ranges of cultural variation between kinesic systems,
but he should, early in his training, undertake at least some
short-time research into kinemorphology. Kinemorphology is the
systematic analysis of patterns of kines. No kine ever stands
alone. Although the novelist may make a point concerning the
interrelationship of two actors by saying, "She winked at him",

such a statement is meaningful only because the reader "fills in" the remainder of the system. There are a variety of kinds of "winks.". We may experimentally isolate a series of these "winks" and see that the difference between them is examinable quite apart from the meaning context in which they occur. In the example above, the verbal context plus the empathetic sub-visual acting of the reader supplies the modiying and quali-fying kines, which accompany the particular kine, which re-late to the lowering of one lid (at an implied stress and velo-city) while holding the other relatively immobile, but open.

In setting up kinemorphs from "raw" kines, we may pro-ceed experimentally by using a systematic contrast series either in a laboratory with an actor or in "nature." This series is recorded at a variety of times in a variety of situations in order to check for systematic variation.

In the laboratory situation the following procedure is recommended. An informant is used whose instructions are to answer but one question. "Does this 'mean' something differ-ent than this?" In the study of kinemorphics an informant cannot be expected to tell you what a given pattern means. He is only equipped to tell you that within his system of diakines one kinemorph means something different than another. If the student is skilled in motion projection, that is, if he can imagine situations and project these kinesically or, better, can have enough control so that he can "set" a pat-tern of kines and hold them for reaction, he can record the response variations. If he cannot project motion, one of two devices should be used. He should get an actor to whom he can hand written instructions, or, and this may be the device which will be developed later for training purposes, he may present the informant with a series of pictures and request information concerning similarities and differences.

It must be recalled that we are in kinemorphic research seeking meaningful kines and that our research is designed to lead us to an understanding of the significance of a given kine in a given pattern. Significance is here being measured not by what is meant by the particular pattern and pattern variation but "does the variation of a particular kine change the meaning of the particular pattern?" In other words, we are concerned here not with the extent or degree or kind of difference in activity stimulated by one set of kines as against another. We are concerned with the variation in the kines with-in a kinemorph which make for some kind of difference in res-ponse. Such meaning will hereafter be described as differential.

Kinemorphs, methodologically speaking, are of two varieties. The example given above of the "wink" represents one in which there is a base kine as defined explicitly by the particular culture (these are commonly called "gestures"). There are many of these, and the student is urged to work with them during his initial sensitization program. Other examples might be the "handshake", the "nod", "foot pat", "frown", etc.. The second variety can be discovered only through empirical investigation and by the careful study of raw data. It is my opinion that many kinemorphs exist without a culturally-defined base kine. These, which might be described as the "unknown base kinemorphs", will undoubtedly loom very important in the examination of the kinesic systems of societies other than that of the speaker and in the investigation of the particular constructs of the idiokinesic system.

In order to illustrate the isolation of kinemorphs, the base kine "wink" will be utilized. Before demonstrating the analysis of kinemorphic activity, several statements concerning methodological theory should be stated. For purposes of investigation the body has been divided into a series of areas:

1.	Total head	5.	Shoulder-arm-wrist
2.	Face	6.	Hand
3.	Neck	7.	Hip-joint - leg - ankle
4.	Trunk	8.	Foot

A differential meaning pattern or kinemorph in any given area will be described as an act. A combination of any two or more acts is called an action. The reader is warned that the discussion is still dealing with differential and not with contextual meaning. We are still concerned with isolating motion particles and constructions from the total array presented by the human (social) body in an entirely morphological sense.

This involves the abstraction of a series of repetitively appearing motion-particle patterns with significance measured by differential meaning. Analogically, this stage of the research may be related to that of the linguist working with an unanalyzed language, who, having derived sets of repetitive sounds, is seeking the logics of construction in that language. I believe that by this method we are orienting the study of body motion in a direction whereby it will ultimately be possible to analyze contextual meaning empirically, and through scientific experimentation, rather than through the often misleading devices concerning meaning derivation supplied by intuitionist philosophical approaches.

One other methodological note must be added before continuing with the example. In the presentation of the kinegraphs in Section II only two varieties of stress are noted. The first of these, strong, is denoted by the symbol (___); the second, weak, by (o). It is immediately evident that this dichotomy is heuristic and that there probably exists in nature a continuum of stress variations. The fact that most of the kines are left unmarked indicates that thusfar in the research a "normal" has been assumed. "Normal" is a statement of the researcher's own unanalyzable experience and is evidently both egocentric and ethnocentric. Exactly what degree of stress constitutes a "normal" stress still remains unknown. The development of devices whereby varying degrees of stress can be analyzed will certainly be an important part of the research in motion.

At this stage in the research it seems advisable to describe the variations of stress (and frequency) as allokinic, that is, as variations on a pattern. In the examples to follow the allokines will be ignored. To include them at this stage of the research would only tend to mislead the reader into accepting material which has not yet been established empirically. The importance of stress and frequency as related to motion cannot be underestimated. Informants report that "there is some difference" in evident situations. How small a difference is really significant remains to be ascertained experimentally.

In the following example the informant is presented with a set of four kines in one area (the face). The informant is encouraged to ignore other areas in his response. It is evident that it is impossible for the informant to be oblivious to the other patterning since it has been shown experimentally that perception takes place in Gestalten. However, in a short time both actor and informant can develop the ability to isolate their perceptions to a "degree."

Each of these four patterns contains four particles (which the actor is attempting) to project. There are, of course, many other elements present in the face which are not being emphasized (and probably over or under dramatized). If the informant reports these in his differential statement they should be recorded and retested with other informants. However, the four major elements described here are the ones being tested in this situation. We are attempting to discover whether these particular component kines are kinemorphically significant.

No. 1.

$$[\text{O} -; \measuredangle; \ominus; \triangle]$$

a. The left eye is closed while the right remains open.

b. The mouth is held in "normal."

c. The tip of the nose is depressed (bunnynose).

d. The left orbital margin is squinted.

(This projection is held for no more than five seconds.)
(Retest with shorter duration.)

No. 2.

$$[-\text{O};\measuredangle; \ominus; \triangle]$$

a. The right eye is closed while the left remains open.

b. The mouth is held in "normal."

c. The tip of the nose is depressed (bunnynose).

d. The left orbital margin is squinted.

Informants remark: "They look different but they wouldn't mean
anything different."

Tentative analysis: Shift from closing of right eye to left eye
does not shift meaning. Leftness and right-
ness allokinic in this case. Use of uni-
lateral squint unnoticed by informant.

No. 3.

$$[\text{O} -; \ominus; \triangle]$$

a. Left eye is closed while right remains open.

b. The mouth is held in "normal."

c. The tip of the nose is depressed.

d. Neither orbit squinted.

Informants remark: "That's the same as the first one."

Tentative analysis: Squint morphologically insignificant.

No. 4.

$$[\circ -; <; \frown; \bigcirc]$$

a. Left eye is closed while right remains open.

b: The mouth drawn into pout.

c. The tip of the nose depressed.

d. Left orbit squinted. (or unsquinted.)

Informants remark: "Well, that changes things."

Tentative analysis: Mouth position morphologically significant.

There are a variety of variations which can be made on this one kinemorph. In the actual kinemorphic analysis from which this was taken, a series of significant acts were derived. The closing of one eye was morphologically significant. The bunny-nose as used here was not significant (although with other kines it has been isolated as kinemorphically significant). On further retests, squint variation was seen to be significant when the mouth was pouted, but not when the mouth was "normal."

Once a set of acts are isolated and their components analyzed for significance, the researcher should then turn to other body areas to begin the construction of actions as measured by differential meaning. In the kinesic systems of American informants thus far studied, the addition of the head to the face acts has often constituted an action per se. The student is warned at this stage of the research to use the same devices for the examination of head acts. Since the total head is involved, there are not so many components, but an extensive set of significant kinemorphic acts may be involved. (In the case of the head a single kinemorph may constitute an act; at times, a set of nods or shakes or medial movements, or any of these combined in series with or without a terminal bounce, may constitute an act.)

When the kinemorphs of the head are isolated, the student is advised to combine the two sets and again examine for kine-morphic and structural significance. He may discover that in certain situations a given act may reinforce another act. At other times, there may appear a negational situation in which either "ambivalence" or "double negatives" are expressed. He should not be surprised to discover that although within the analysis of an act a given kinemorph has significance, the same kinemorph may become non-significant or, at most mini-mally reinforcing in a larger context. For instance: In the following example the medial frown is repeated (together with a stress situation in a speech event). The total head may or may not be in parallel movement with the repetition of the frown. Some informants report that there is a difference, e.g. "stronger." Others say, "This means the same thing." There may be diakinesic differences expressed here.

$$H - h - h \quad \text{or} \quad \overset{\cdots}{\underset{<}{o \; o}}$$

$$\underline{H} \cdot \underline{H} - \underline{h} - h \quad \text{or} \quad \overset{\cdots}{\underset{L}{o \; o}}$$

$$H - h - h \quad + \quad \overset{o \; o}{\underset{L}{}}$$

A similar procedure should be followed in the analysis and combination of the act morphologies represented by the neck, trunk, long members, hands and feet.

> Smith and Trager have pointed out the simila-rity between this kind of analysis and that done by linguists. It will perhaps make the data presented above more meaningful if we out-line the parallel between the two systems of analysis. If the reader recognizes that both speech and motion are parts of culture and is further willing to assess the relationship be-tween the two systems in their mutual functions in the communication system, he will be more willing to accept the parallel between the for-mal approaches to the sub-contextual data.

Table I

From seminar: Henry Lee Smith, George L. Trager, and Ray Birdwhistell

Linguistics			Kinesics	
Sound			Muscular and skeletal shift	
Phone: Allophone			Kine: Allokine	
Phoneme			(?Kineme?)	
Morph: Allomorph				
Morpheme	Word		Kinemorph	Act
	Construction			Action
	Sentence			Action
Utterance in context			Action in context	

4. Social Kinesics

This section will not attempt any review of the personality, communication, and culture hypotheses which are in the process of being tested by the writer and his students. Suffice it to say that there are indications that whether used directly or projectively, kinesic data will provide both recording and diagnostic tools for either the applied or the "pure" researcher. As an interviewing tool, kinesics has provided a dimension of considerable importance to both the interviewer and the interview analyst.

What I should like to do is to present the reader with three examples of recording situations. These three are all taken in context, one on a bus, the second in a home, and the third on a street corner. In only the second of these was there any direct information other than that supplied by the situation itself. Except insofar as there are regional cultural differences in the United States, these can be described as members of the common American culture. Mother and child (conversation A) spoke with a Tidewater, Virginia accent, as did the three adolescent boys (C). The hostess (B) is a native of Cleveland, Ohio, who has been in Washington since 1945; the guest (B) is from a small Wisconsin town and is presently residing in Chicago.

Both the hostess and the guest could probably be assigned an upper middle class position (as measured by a Warner-type analysis). The adolescents live in a middle-income government-worker neighborhood. The bus route on which the bus event was recorded leads to a similar neighborhood. The way in which the mother and child were dressed was not consistent with the dress of other riders who disembarked (as did the observer) before the mother and child did.

The three adolescents were, as far as could be ascertained from their conversation, in the same grade in high school. Both the hostess and her guest were in their late thirties. The child was about four, while his mother seemed to be about twenty-seven to thirty.

It is immediately evident that even in the mother-child and adolescent situation the dress, mannerisms, and situation present a number of cues which would make the social analysis of these kinesic situations somewhat less than blind. The research and general social experience of the recorder obviously have played a selective role in all three situations.

The reader is urged to see that this is a demonstration of the contributory role of kinesic recording. As stated, no kine, act, or action carries social meaning in and of itself. Social meaning appears in a total context. That context extends not only over the total situation in which the observation takes place, but through the perceptual-conceptual system of the recorder and the analyst.

This last may seem to be an unnecessary stricture. However, it has been my experience that there is a great temptation to ask the question, "What does this (a given act or action) mean?" as though symbols came encapsulated with "meaning." The fact that "gesture" has seemed so explicit has contributed to this. More serious is the psychologistic tendency to assume a theory of prior causation to emotional expression and then to attach symbolic significance to the act, verbal or kinesic, as though the "deep" meaning were imminently carried.

To return to the three examples. They are chosen for several reasons. All are familiar events. The particular activity may vary from general middle class American experience, but the general form is repetitive and makes the introspective recognition of the context less difficult. In all three of these events there is systematic development of the situation which would permit relatively easy analysis. Finally, all three of these are "scenes"; that is, in the dramatic sense, there is a start and a finish which enables us to "tie the situation down."

5. Sample Conversations With Description.

Conversation A. Mother-child (Four-year old boy) event.

Observed on bus (Arlington, Va. to Washington, D. C.), April 14, 1952. Analyzed (with H. L. Smith, Jr. and G. L. Trager) on April 15, 1952.

Stress and intonation are indicated above the pertinent text, using the symbols provided in Trager and Smith's Outline of English Structure, Studies in Linguistics, Occasional Papers 3, 1951; voice-qualifiers, e.g. the drawl (⌒), are indicated by symbols developed by the above authors in as yet unpublished material. Kinesic symbols are below the pertinent text. In a few places a phonemic transcription of the text is also provided, according to Trager and Smith's analysis.

The kinesic symbols are translated verbally, for the convenience of the reader, on the pages immediately following each conversation.

26.

Data:

1. Child: Mama. I gotta go to the bathroom.

2. Mother: 3-3-3

3. Child: Mama. Donnie's gotta go.
   R 35
   no R sleeve

4. Mother: Sh-sh.
   R 5 across child's lap - firm through5

5. Child: But mama.
   XX4

6. Mother: Later. (o openness; over-softness)

7. Child: mah / mah (over-loudness; whine)
   Mama.
   R 5   against mo. thigh
   no Arm

8. Mother: Wait. (rasp)
   R 14   against child's thighs

9. Child: Oh mama, mama, mama.
   H   H

10. Mother: Shut up. Will yuh.
    L 35 child's L. U. arm behind
          own R. arm

7. - Juncture markers |, \\, and # should be on a line with the pitch numbers (this applies everywhere on this page and p.29 and p.32).

Erratum

Description:

1. This situation was observed on a street bus at about 2:30 P.M., April 14. The little boy was seated next to the window. He seemed tired of looking out the window and, after surveying all of the car ads and the passengers, he leaned toward his mother and pulled at her sleeve, pouted and vigorously kicked his legs.

2. The mother had been sitting erectly in her seat, her packages on her lap, and her hands lightly clasped around the packages. She was apparently "lost in thought."

3. When the boy's initial appeal failed to gain the mother's attention, he began to jerk at her sleeve again, each jerk apparently stressing his vocalization.

4. The mother turned and looked at him, "shushed" him, and placed her right hand firmly across his thighs.

5. The boy protested audibly; clenched both fists, pulled them with stress against his chest. At the same time he drew his legs up against the restraint of the mother's hand. His mouth was drawn down and his upper face was pulled into a tight frown.

6. The mother withdrew her hand from his lap and resettled in her former position with her hands clasped around the packages.

7. The boy grasped her upper arm tightly, continued to frown. When no immediate response was forthcoming, he turned and thrust both knees into the lateral aspect of her left thigh.

8. She looked at him, leaned toward him, and slapped him across the anterior portion of his upper legs.

9. He began to jerk his clenched fists up and down, vigorously nodding between each inferior-superior movement of his fists.

10. She turned, frowning, and with her mouth pursed, she spoke to him through her teeth. Suddenly she looked around, noted that other passengers were

watching, forced a square smile. At the same
time that she finished speaking, she reached
her right hand in under her left arm and squeezed
the boy's arm. He sat quietly.

Data:

Conversation B: Hostess-guest event.

    Observed April 17, 1952; analyzed (with G. L. Trager)
on April 18.

Introductory note: Guest of honor forty-five minutes late.
                   Three couples waiting, plus host and
                   hostess. Host had arranged guest list
                   for function.

1.   Hostess: Oh, we were afraid you werent coming, but good,

2.   Guest: Im very sorry, get held up, you know calls

         and all that,

3.   Hostess: Put your wraps here, People are dying to

         meet you, Ive told them all about you,

4.   Guest: You have well I dont know, Yes, Ho, I'd love

         Clutches coat

         to meet them,

Description:

1. As the hostess opened the door to admit her guest, she smiled a closed-toothed smile. As she began speaking she drew her hands, drawn into loose fists, up between her breasts. Opening her eyes very wide, she then closed them slowly and held them closed for several words. As she began to speak she dropped her head to one side and then moved it toward the guest in a slow sweep. She then pursed her lips momentarily before continuing to speak, nodded, shut her eyes again, and spread her arms, indicating that he should enter.

2. He looked at her fixedly, shook his head, and spread his arms with his hands held open. He then began to shuffle his feet and raised one hand, turning it slightly outward. He nodded, raised his other hand, and turned it palm-side up as he continued his vocalization. Then he dropped both hands and held them, palms forward, to the side and away from his thighs. He continued his shuffling.

3. She smiled at him, lips pulled back from clenched teeth. Then, as she indicated where he should put his coat, she dropped her face momentarily into an expressionless pose. She smiled toothily again, clucked and slowly shut, opened, and shut her eyes again as she pointed to the guest with her lips. She then swept her head from one side to the other. As she said the word "all" she moved her head in a sweep up and down from one side to the other, shut her eyes slowly again, pursed her lips, and grasped the guest's lapel.

4. The guest hunched his shoulders, which pulled his lapel out of the hostess's grasp. He held his coat with both hands, frowned, and then blinked rapidly as he slipped the coat off. He continued to hold tightly to his coat.

Data:

Conversation C: Adolescent meeting.

Observed April 20, 1952. Analyzed (with H. L. Smith, Jr.) on April 21.

Introductory note: Two boys (1 and 2, 14-16 years old) approach third (3) same age leaning against drugstore window   one foot   against base of window.

1. Boy 1:   Hiyah#

2. Boy 3:   Hiyah#   Whatcha doing#

3. Boy 1:   Piggin#   What cha doing#

4. Boy 3:   Waitin for the guys#

5. Boy 1:   This is Jep Smithers#   Jus moved inta the

   village#   From Richmond#

32.

6.   Boy 3:   Hiyah#

7.   Boy 2:   Hiyah#

8.   Boy 3:   What year ya in#

9.   Boy 2:   First   Junior#

10. Boy 3:   Play football

11. Boy 2:   Well   I was sick for a coupla years#

12. Boy 3:   Oh

Description:

1. This observation was made at 5:00 P.M. April 20.
Two adolescent boys (1 and 2) walked up to a drugstore window against which leaned a third of about
the same age. One of the boys (1) leaned one foot
against the window and looked out at the street.
He turned his eyes toward the original occupant
(3) of the window, spoke, and then looked back at
the street. He shoved both hands deep in his pants
pockets.

2. Boy (3) turned briefly toward them. Then he looked
out at the street, put his left hand in his pants
pocket, his right hand in his side coat pocket.
Withdrawing his left hand with a cigarette and a
lighter in it, he put the cigarette in his mouth,
lit it and closed the lighter with a snap. Then he
slowly blew a cloud of smoke toward the street.

3. Turning his head toward the other, boy 1 slowly
raised and lowered one eyebrow. He put both feet
on the ground and stood with his legs widely spread.
Continuing to look at the other boy (3), he tucked
his thumbs under his belt and very slowly lifted
the front of his trousers, shook them, and then
dropped them into place.

4. Boy 3 looked at boy 2, stuck out his lower lip,
and slowly blew smoke at him. Then he looked
casually at the boy (2) who had accompanied the
original speaker.

5. Noting the interest in the boy that had accompanied
him to the corner, boy 1 at the same time jerked
his thumb, cocked his head, and gestured with the
corner of his mouth toward him. He pointed toward
a row of apartments across the street and then made
his face expressionless throughout the remainder of
his vocalization.

6. Boy 3 raised one eyebrow and held his cigarette in
the right hand corner of his mouth. After speaking
he rolled it to the left side of his mouth and blew
out a cloud of smoke.

7. Boy 2 looked at boy 3, stuck out his hand as though to shake hands, withdrew it when there was no response and stuck it "over-casually" into his pocket, blinked rapidly, and then quickly licked his lips.

8. Boy 3 looked at boy 2, blinked, and nodded his head.

9. Boy 2 looked at the street and frowned.

10. Boy 3 raised one eyebrow, nodded, moved his head slowly from one side to another. Then he quickly removed his foot from the window sill, pretended to kick an imaginary football. Then he pretended to pass the football, turned around quickly, stooped and pretended to catch a ball thrown to him.

11. Boy 2 blinked several times and shuffled his feet, dropped his head and moved it to one side. Frowning, he held out his right hand palm up and then turned it over palm down.

12. Boy 3 looked out at the street with his face held expressionless.

Section II: KINEGRAPHS.

The notational system demonstrated below divides the body into eight major sections. Inasmuch as most of the writer's research experience has been with American sub-cultures, these reflect his own ethnocentrism. The fact that he has had some opportunity to observe members of other national and ethnic groups here, in Mexico, and in Canada, and has spent some time in the field with two American Indian groups, may lessen this ethnocentrism, but it still remains. Until other workers take this or a similar recording system into the field and specifically study the motion systems of other peoples we must continue to suspect our data.

This is reflected in the evident lack of stress on intra-trunk muscles, neck, and foot activity. Most of the recording and research upon which this orthography is based has been done in clothed cultures.

This system is organized in such a way that it can be easily expanded. It is hoped that any student reading this who thinks of other kines or evident organizations of kines will communicate with the author in order that they can be listed.

It will be noted that this is a relatively static system. Only in the area of the long members is there much stress laid on movement. It is my hope that forthcoming research using motion pictures will make it possible to develop techniques which will make this more dynamic. The success of linguistics and phonetics in operating with the use of "stationary particle" recording gives some justification to the present system.

I am dissatisfied with the terminology employed for the description of types of walking, but in the absence of mobile visual aid material, the concepts used, in spite of their value-loading, have proved quite useful, with minimal involvement.

The eight sections into which the body is divided represent an arbitrary classification system which may be abandoned later. However, it has proved useful for the groups recorded thus far.

35.

Body Sections and Base Symbol

1. **Total head:** (H h ℛ)

2. **Face:**   The selection of facial "parts" evidently re-
   flects Western European emphases: (Symbols
   are pictographs of facial features) ⌣ Δ

3. **Trunk:**   To be considerably expanded as observations
   of pectoral, stomach, and back muscles are
   analyzed in context. (ʒ ʃ T Y   ).

4. **Shoulder, arm, and wrist:** This section must be expanded
   to indicate muscle signals as they are lo-
   cated. Particularly must careful experimental
   work be done in localizing flows and avoidances
   of tension, of inception, and extension of
   activity. ⊬ ⟨ ⅃

5. **Hand and finger activity:** This complex system of numerical
   recording will be even further expanded when
   the data from more highly flexible cultures
   are added. (Numbers from 1 - 5)

6. **Hip, leg, ankle:**   See Shoulder, arm, and wrist
   (alphabetical notation of joints) ⅄ ∥

7. **Foot activity, walking:**   The extent of foot covering present in the research situations so far have
   limited the kinegraphic isolation. (By addition of T before numbers, finger recording
   can easily be translated into toe and foot
   recording.)

8. **Neck:**   The relatively few kines listed below for
   neck kines again reflect Western European
   observation situations. It is probable that
   as Indonesian and other neck-active cultures
   are observed that a more extensive orthography must be developed. ∥

Utilizing this basic notational logic, the system has the advantage that it can be easily learned and may be extensively expanded.

The reader is urged to learn quickly the following "through space" indicants.

↑   - To a superior position

↓   - To an inferior position

⟶   - To an anterior position

⟵   - To a posterior position

↷   - To a lateral position (use R or L to indicate direction)

↶   - To a medial position

⟶| - Indicates continuity of any particular motion or position

1. Total Head.

"Norm"	Stress	Oversoft	Variants	
H	H	H	H H H	Full nod up and down or down and up
h	h	h	h h h	Half nod either up or down
h	h	h	h h h	Small "bounce"* at end of H or h (in its variations)
		fx		Tense medial multiple nod, usually alone
		fx		Same over soft
H	H	H	H H H	Full side and back sweep (May contain nod or half nod)
h	h	h	h h h	Half sweep (May contain nod or half nod)
h	h	h	h h h	Small bounce at end of H or h (in its variations)
		fx		Tense medial multiple sweep usually alone

* "Bounce" is a bad term if taken literally. Head and neck muscles not necessarily in strain.

"Norm"	Stress	Oversoft	Variants	
				Same oversoft
				Cooked head

2. Face.

Blank faced

Single raised brow ⌒ indicates brow raised

Lowered brow

Medial brow contraction

Medial brow nods

Raised brows

Wide eyed

Wink

Lateral squint

Full squint

Shut eyes (with A-closed pause 2 count
Blink ⟶   B-closed pause 5 plus count

Side wise look

Focus on auditor

Stare

Rolled eyes

Slitted eyes

Eyes upward

Shifty eyes

Glare

Inferior lateral orbit contraction

Curled nostril

Flaring nostrils

Pinched nostrils

Bunny-nose

Nose wrinkle

Left sneer

Right sneer

Out of the side of the mouth (left)

Out of the side of the mouth (right)

Set jaw

Smile   tight-- loose o

Mouth in repose   lax o - tense —

Droopy mouth

Tongue in cheek

Pout

Clenched teeth

Toothy smile

Square smile

⊚	Open mouth
S⊚L	Slow lick – lips
Q⊚L	Quick lick – lips
∽	Moistening lips
⊲	Lip biting
☺	Whistle
☼	Pursed lips
☼	Retreating lips
☼→	Peck
☼!	Smack
▱	Lax mouth
☒	Chin protruding
☞	"Dropped" jaw

44.

⊢X-X⊣ Chewing

Temples tightened

ε Ʒ Ear "wiggle"

Total scalp movement

3. Trunk and Shoulders

Spine (Profile)

Upright - lax - (or supported in chair) an imaginary line dropped perpendicular from spine of first thoracic vertebrae would intersect sacrum.

Upright ("stiff")

Anterior spinal curvature, thorax upright but lax, lumbar-sacral region thrust anteriorly. (If seated, buttocks firm on seat).

Anterior spinal curvature, thorax upright but lax, sacral region thrust anteriorly. (Seated on posterior aspect of the sacrum.)

Sacral region upright, thorax thrust forward, upright.

Anterior slump.

"Rared back."

Lean back.

Lean forward.

In all kinegraphs concerning spine — indicates tension, ○ indicates overrelaxation.

Spine (Frontal)

Upright - lax - (or supported in chair)
An imaginary line dropped perpendicularly
from spine of first thoracic vertebrae would
intersect sacrum.

Curvature right.

Curvature left.

Lean right.

Lean left.

     The following applies to both profile and frontal views
of the spine.

Curvature beginning at base of thorax.

Curvature beginning at sacro-illiac.

Curvature beginning at buttocks (i.e. involves hip axis)

Shoulders

T   Straight - lax -∘   ——   for "stiff."

Y   Hunched shoulders

Y   Shrug __ for stress.   Line following indi-
                                               cates duration ⌐

T   Left shoulder raised.

T   Right shoulder raised.

↑   Drooped (lateral) shoulders.

T   Single drooped (lateral) shoulder (left).

T   Single drooped (lateral) shoulder (right).

T^   Left shoulder forward. (Add P under right
           wing if right shoulder retreats coterminously.)

^T   Right shoulder forward. (add P under left
           wing if left shoulder retreats coterminously.)

T°   Left shoulder back.

°T   Right shoulder back.

Ŧ^   Left anterior thorax twist.

^Ŧ   Right anterior thorax twist.

Ŧ^   Left anterior trunk twist (from sacro illiac)

太	Right anterior trunk twist (from sacro-illiac)
ㅔ	Cupped shoulders.
ᅮ	Shoulders back.

Pectoral muscles

T	Left pectoral tense
T	Right pectoral tense
T	Chest tension
T	Chest overlax

Stomach muscles

击	Stomach tense
击	Stomach flaccid
声	Stomach protruded
声	Stomach sucked in
击	Left stomach tense
击	Right stomach tense

4. Shoulder, Arm and Wrist

Note: Recording of Shoulder-Upper arm, Upper arm-Lower arm, Lower arm-wrist, uni-lateral or bi-lateral, requires considerable experience in observation. However, considerable practice (with a checking observer) can equip the recorder with sufficient facility and accuracy to meet most problems in general posture. Movement is still more difficult and the student is urged to practice "seeing in space" before trusting his records.

Warning: Musculature and jointing are both involved in the analysis of long member activity. Most Americans assume constant parallel activity of these two interdependent physiological systems. Muscular tension does not necessarily flow from a medial point of inception to the most distant point. Nor does a similar movement of skeletal structure always involve the same muscles in tension orientation.

Shoulder (and/or) arm skeletal

#0	Chest and shoulder inceptual activity
#1	Upper arm from caput to elbow
#2	Tip of radius-ulnar complex to wrist
#3	Wrist-upper hand activity
R #0123	Activity (posture or movement) of right shoulder-arm-wrist
R #01	Activity (posture or movement) of right shoulder-upper arm angle
R #23	Activity (posture or movement) of right lower arm and wrist of hand

Either of two angle recording systems may be employed.
Either degree of angle recorded as ∠ 30, 45, etc. or a clock
system employed. Practice with a protractor (oversize) can
sensitize observer to degree of ∠ but this takes considerable
practice. If Air Force experience can be taken here, the
clock system seems practical and more easily learned. It is
this which will be emphasized below.

The plane of the superior or medial member is used as the
base plane. The angle formed by the shoulder plane when the
upper arm is extended directly above the head is recorded R #01
(M). Movements or postures from (M) are counted clockwise.
Thus when the upper arm is extended directly medial, lateral,
or anterior in the shoulder plane is recorded as R #01 (3) ...
direction is indicated by arrows: ⌒ indicating medial
point. ⌒ indicating lateral point. ⟶ indicating anterior point.

R #01 (3) ⟶   Figure shown indicates: right upper
                arm extended directly anteriorly from
                the shoulder.

R #01 (6)   Figure shown indicates: upper arm lax
                extended directly down from shoulder.
                (6 and M require no arrows).

Note: For rapid recording only M to 6 is necessary.
Arrows indicate mediality or laterality of gesture. Also
posterior or anterior movement. R and L always recorded.

Motion clock

M
1   1

2   2

3   3

4   4

5   5

6

Following the same logic, the plane of upper arm is used to assess lower arm upper arm.

R #12 (M)   Regardless of relationship of up-
                                   per arm to shoulder this signifies
                                   the closest proximity of lower arm
                                   plane to upper arm plane.

R #12 (3)   Upper arm and lower arm at right
                                   angles. Use arrows to indicate
                                   point.

Note: Logic continues in recording wrist angle.

R #23 (6)   Hand extended to continue lower arm
                                   line.

R #23 (3)   Hand at right angles to arm line.

Note: As recorded above ╱ is seen as anterior or posterior break at wrist. If articulation is to lateral rather than medial portion of the wrist, record as follows:

R #23 (2 ul) ⟶   Right wrist ╱ at 2 o'clock, break
R #23 (2 ra) ⟶   toward ulnar side; point; lateral.

Note: In the recording of lower arm movements it is at times significant to record the direction of the twist of the arm. Recorder should follow below:

R #2 (ul ⟶)   or R #2 (ul ⟵)   Indicating twist at upper-
or R #2 (ul ⤳) or R #2 (ul ↜)   arm lower arm break (elbow)
or R #2 (ul ↑) or R #2 (ul ↓)   with direction of ulnar
                                   region.

Note: To indicate tension or laxity of muscles of shoulder or arm section underline arm recording wherever tension occurs. Thus

R #01 (3 ⟶)#12(6) #23(6)(ul⤳)1111   Right arm extended,
                                     lax, directly ante-
                                     rior ulnar portion
                                     medial, fingers ex-
                                     tended lax, utilizing
                                     tension in the lower
                                     arm for lift and sus-
                                     pension.

or

R ≠01 (5 ⤸)#12(1) #23(6)(ul→) 1 3 1   Upper arm at five
                (table)   (cheek)   o'clock, elbow
                                           sharply bent to one
                                           o'clock, hand ex-
                                           tended tense from
                                           the wrist, thumb
                                           hooked, three medial
                                           fingers extended
                                           stiff pushing against
                                           cheek with A, little
                                           finger hooked. Note
                                           sub-line notations
                                           indicating pressure
                                           points against table
                                           and cheek.

Bi-membral activity

If arms are in complementary activity representing same
activity use double # sign: ##, otherwise record separately
using R# signal and L# signal prefixing notation.

XX01 (6)#12(3 ⇌) 23(6)(ul ↓ ;XX1)   Fingers intertwined,
            (chairarms)   arms loosely held
                                         across stomach, el-
                                         bow end of ulnar por-
                                         tion of lower arm
                                         resting on chair.

Note: The use of arrows within the brackets or parentheses
indicates direction of placement, such usage follows segment signal. In order to portray motion, use arrows on line above signal
recording. If all of arm is included in the motion:

R# 0123   Indicating motion of hand and arm
                                 with shoulder activity moving from
                                 zero position to a lateral position.

R# 1 #2 - #3   Indicates ordinal movement beginning
                                 with upper arm followed by lower arm
                                 and hand. Initial movement lateral
                                 with upper arm, followed by anterio-
                                 lateral sweep with lower arm, upper
                                 arm remaining in position.

It may be seen that considerable practice with symbols is required before recorder can use the full numerical system of orthography. Therefore the following is recommended in original recording situation. Two figures are conceived, one shaped ▢ , the other ❘ . These represent respectively a face view of the trunk and a lateral view. Note that the clock system is still used to record ∠.

This figure represents the upper body set of a person sitting in a chair, elbows resting on the arms and with his head held up by the fingers pressing against the cheek.

The above illustration indicates that at times it may be necessary to have more space for recording the 01, 12, 23 series. Since most of the recording and analysis of body activity will necessarily be done one area at a time it will not impede work to any real extent if an entire page is assigned to the schematic drawing of the trunk and its extensions. Several examples will be shown of long member recording on the page to follow. The use of graph paper with pre drawn base figures has proved efficient as a recording device. If the recorder has learned his angle clock sufficiently well, the fact that he cannot draw is relatively unimportant since he will have the angles and the tension points in reproducable terms. If he can draw, and I have seen few students who cannot be quickly trained to draw these simple line figures, his figure will assist him in his notations and recall later.

It must be remembered that in all cases these kines have a dual purpose. The first of these concerns actual morphological research and second as a mnemonic aid. Motion research, particularly once it is related to the interview or contextual observation situation must be recalled and written up like any other interview where verbalization is stressed. It has been my experience that a sensitive interviewer can get rather complete recall with such notations. Any "written" notes that the observer can take along with his kinegraphic recording should be added.

5. Hand and finger activity.

A. Ball of finger.
a. Tip of finger.
(A), (B), (C), and (O) indicates back
 of finger or hand.

In notating, when particular finger
is under discussion, list in the following order:

Hand: (R) or (L)
Finger: 1, 2, 3, 4, 5, or) for palm
        of hand.
Action: Hook, (or reverse; hyper-ex-
        tension), Curl, or Closure.
Points of contact: With thumb as 1,
        maintain ordinality 1A-2B, 2A-3
        (B), 4-5 translates "The ball
        of the thumb contacting the se-
        cond joint of the forefinger,
        the first joint of which is con-
        tacting the posterior aspect of
        the second joint of the middle
        finger; the fourth and little
        finger being laterally separated
        from the middle finger and main-
        taining contact with each other
        laterally along the entire joint
        plane."

In notating, when entire hand is under
consideration, the particular finger
need not be listed. List in the following order:

Hand: (R) or (L)
Finger pattern: See below, remembering
        that all notation starts with
        the thumb as initial 1.

Finger

(L) | Extended (lax).

(L) | Extended, tense.

(L) ⌐   Hyper-extended, posterior crook.

(L) 2,3,4,5 —⌃—   Posteriorly patterned multi-angle
(Until otherwise shown,
angle sketch conveys suf-
ficient variation.)

(L) 1, 2, etc.   Hook, tip of involved joint (a) con-
tracted no further than B-c
line of acting finger.

(L) 1, 2, etc.   Curl, tip of involved joint (a) con-
tracted beyond inferior C line
but not touching palm at any
point.

(L) 1₀, 2₀, etc.   Closure (lax) (excepting thumb, Fl.)
tip touching palm.

(L) 1₀, 2₀, etc.   Closure (tense) (excepting thumb, Fl.)
tip touching palm.

(L) 1□, 2□, etc.
1⊕, 2⊙, etc.   Touching object. Pressure indicated by
— and ○ .

(L) †, ⸕, etc.   Grasping object. Pressure indicated by
— and ○ .

(L) 1□, 2□
1⊕, 2⊕   Finger caress. Pressure indicated by
" and . To indicate in-
volved joint, ordinality pattern:
Hand: (L) or (R).
Finger number.
Anterior or posterior crook signa
Joint signal.
Pressure stress.
Stationary object sign: □
Movable object sign: ⊕

(L) I𝖝 , 2𝖝,etc.

Finger drumming. Intensity and duration indicated by ___ . ___

(L) Ⓘ

Encircling of symbol indicates posterior aspect of the finger in
any of the above.

(L) Y̆

Indicates (apparent) autonomy of finger or joint.

Total Hand

(L) |||||

Hand extended, (lax). No finger touching another.

(L) |||||

Hand extended, (tense). No fingers
touching.

(L) 5

Hand extended, lax or tense (tension
indicated by ___ Fingers each
touching neighboring finger.

(L) |3|

First finger not touching second; second,
third, and fourth touching along
length; fifth finger not touching
others. This logic may be followed as in 41, 311, 23, 122 etc.

(L) ⌐1₂3₃

All crooking notation follows logic
shown above for single fingers.
Figure shown illustrates "Thumb
(1) crooked posteriorly and not
touching other fingers; fingers
3, 4, and 5 touching along length
and with a curl; finger two (2)
not touching with a tense hook.

(L) 1 ²³₃

Notation for joint touching is placed
over the numerical finger-indica-
ting figure. Figure shown illustrates: 1 extended (lax); 2 ᶜ
touching 3 at joints B and C, with
2 extended (lax); 3, 4, 5 touching
along length and in curl.

(L) ┼┤

Fist (lax), thumb outside over fingers
2, 3. (In this case conventionality eliminates necessity for
1's contact points on posterior
portions of 2 and 3). Tense indicated by ___ .

(L) $\widehat{14}$ Capped fist, thumb continuing radial
line and touching 1A to 2BC.
(Conventionality eliminates
necessity for noting 1's contact points on 2's joints.)
Tense indicated by   .

(L) 4   Fist with fingers wrapped around thumb.
(Conventionality eliminates
necessity for noting contact
points.)

(L) 5 □   Full hand grasp of immovable object.

(L) 5 ⊕   Full hand grasp of movable object.

(L) 35   Radial grasp.

(L) 53   Ulnar grasp.

(L) 14 ⊣   Pull, involving 2345.

(L) ||||| or (((((Cupped hand, fingers not touching
neighboring fingers. Direc-
tion of U indicates superior
or inferior direction of palm.

(L) 5̆ or 5̂   Cupped hand, fingers touching neighboring fingers. (U usage same
as above).

(L) 5   Hand at rest, all fingers touching on
another part of own body.*

(L) |||||̆   Autonomic hand.

*Experience shows that written notation of body part touched, e.g.
(knee) avoids confusion.

↑ =
5 (etc.)   ↓ =
5 (etc.)

Indicates superior or inferior motion of hand. Arrow indicates direction. ___ and ● indicates pace.**

⤴5 =   ⤵5 =

Indicates lateral or medial movement of the hand. Arrow indicates direction. ___ and ○ indicates pace.**

→5   or   ⌒‖‖‖
∩   ∩

Indicates anterior or posterior motion of the hand. Arrow indicates direction. ___ and ● indicates pace.

Combinations of the above may be superimposed on each other (follows hand identification pattern). Illustration shows a laterally (to right) anteriorly moving cupped right hand, palms down.

⌒→
3 5

Ulnar cupping or semi-cupping (in motion).

⌒←
5 3

Radial cupping or semi-cupping (in motion).

→
ɔ-A
2 3

"Okay" sign. Illustration shows tip of (1a) 1 touching ball of 2 (2A) while 3, 4, and 5 touch each other and are extended lightly. Note ordinality of motion direction.

A-   ɔ⌒ɔ
     1 3 1

B-   ɔ⌒β
     1 2 1 1

C-   A-BB
     3 1, 1

A., B., C., are illustrations of notating joint contacts when total hand is under notation.

** Only necessary when wrist, elbow, and shoulder angles (see below) are not shown.

Bi-Manual.

One of the most important avenues of research in kinesics will probably be that of assessing degrees and situationality of bi-manuality. The bimanualities listed here are restricted to some of those in which the hands are brought into close proximity with each other. This carries certain somatic-space assumptions which undoubtedly will be reoriented as research proceeds.

(14)(14)

Reflexive hand shake, utilizing thumb as base for either hand, R1AB curling with pressure over posterior aspects of the hand; the base of L1B making firm contact with lateral aspect of 2C and depending on thumb length, 3C and 4C; 2345 are firmly touching along length and curl around the posterior aspect of the opposing hand. This may be reversed with left hand in superior position. Note: movement from a medial to an inferior position and return. Variant; (rare) hands may be held in same plane as head and move anterior and return.

$$RL IX 4X \overset{M}{\underset{\downarrow}{\uparrow}}$$

or

$$RL \overset{M}{IX} 4X$$

Reflexive hand hold: Right hand in primary grasp position: R1 curling around posterior aspect of L2C and 3C, R2, 3, 4, 5, curled around posterior ulnar aspect of right hand, held by R1 which is again held by L1 which curls over 1BC. May be held at rest or held in head plane (lateral) and moved in an anterio-posterior set of movements. May be reversed.

$$RL IO XX$$

Intermembral handhold: Firm clasp of interlaced fingers with (as illustrated R in superior position) intermembral contacts marked by joint notation (ill. Cs) and with degree of finger flexion or extension marked by crook signs.

$$R5 \overset{3}{L5} \quad or \quad R5 \overset{A}{L5}$$

Finger-tip hand hold: Tips or balls of all fingers in oppositional contact.

$R5^{\textbf{2}} L5^{\textbf{x}}$ or $R5^{A} L5^{A}$

Finger-tip hand ball: Tips or balls of all fingers touching. C aspect of palms also touching in opposition.

$IXI\land 6XX$

Bi-manual steepling: In this case R1B presses posterior aspect of L1B in XX pattern as are the paired 3, 4, 5; R2A touches L2A in bi-lateral extension.

$14\overline{2}41$

Four-fingered grooving: R2, 3, 4, 5 slide in and out (or rest) touching lateral complimentary member of L2, 3, 4, 5. As shown R1 and L1 are laxly extended but not touching R2BC which can be indicated by marking 1's with crooks. Note variant in motion with medio-lateral arrows.

$I(8)XXI$

Inverted four fingered intermembral handhold: L2, 3, 4, 5 and R2, 3, 4, 5 are interlaced; R1 and L1 remain laxly extended; palms upward. Fingers touching posterior aspect of hand.

$I(8)XXI$

Four fingered intermembral handhold: same as above, palms down. Fingers touching posterior aspect of hand.

$IX3_{2} IX3_{2}$

Limited intermembral handhold: As illustrated R1 crosses L1; R234 curl behind L2 to posterior aspect; L2 touches and crosses R5; R5 touches L3; L3, 4, 5 remain free (note crook) touching each other. This can be varied for particular interlace pattern.

$I_{o}4_{o}><I_{o}4_{o}$

Each hand firmly grips complimentary wrist.

$I8XXI$

Cupped interlace: Similar to four-fingered intermembral handhold except that posterior aspects of R and L 2, 3, 4, 5 rest within bi-manual palms.

A. $R5\overline{5}5$
B. $L5\overline{4}5$

Right Hand Wring: A. - Right hand strips left hand with fingerward movement involving ulnar-radial or radial ulnar twist. Can be reversed to Left Hand Wring; B.

Bi-manual Hand-Wring.

RL5+5

Double-four hook: R2, 3, 4, 5 curled into L5, 4, 3, 2; L1 and R1 extended (lax).

14 ☺ 41

Nail picking:

$\frac{23}{1}$

$\overset{\rightarrow\leftarrow}{55}$

Double five clap: Motion latero-medial; Intensity indicated by ___ or ○ . Duration indicated by ......

$\overset{\rightarrow\leftarrow}{14\ 5}$

One thumb clap: Same as above except one hand slightly turned to free thumb from direct contact.

$\overset{\rightarrow\leftarrow}{O\ o+}$

Double-palm clap (side): Superior-inferior - inferior-superior, latero-medial motion.

$\overset{\rightarrow\leftarrow}{14\ 41}$

Double-four clap: L2, 3, 4, 5 slapping across R2, 3, 4, 5. Can be inverted.

$\overset{\rightarrow\leftarrow}{14\ O}$

Four on the palm clap: L or R 2, 3, 4, 5 on complimentary palm.

$\overset{\rightarrow\leftarrow}{14\ O+}$

Side 4 on the palm clap: Same as four on the palm except that fingers strike across rather than parallel with the palm.

$\overset{\rightarrow\leftarrow}{o\ o}$

Double palm clap: Palm to palm, fingers hyper-extended avoiding contact.

$\frac{5}{5}$ or $\begin{matrix}5\\5\\\mathfrak{D}\end{matrix}$

Hand rubbing: Position of ⌐ indicates superior position

॥॥॥ O ॥॥॥

Extended thumb wave: Thumb directed medially, ulnar aspect of the hand anterior and/or inferior, L or R1a contacting lateral ulnar aspect of B portion of palm, R2, 3, 4, 5 moving in complimentary fashion to L2, 3, 4, 5

Note: →○ (above numeral) indicates one hand at rest → ← both hands moving.

6. Hip, upper leg, lower leg, ankle.

Note: Recording of Shoulder-upper arm, upper arm-lower arm, lower arm-wrist, uni-lateral or bi-lateral, require considerable experience in observation. Considerable practice, with the aid of a checking observer, can equip the recorder with sufficient facility and accuracy to meet problems in general posture. Movement is still more difficult and the student is urged to practice "seeing in space" before trusting his records.

> Warning: Musculature and jointing (skeletal activity) are both involved in the analysis of long member activity. Most Americans interviewed assume constant parallel activity between the muscular and the skeletal system. Muscular tension does not necessarily flow from a medial point of inception to the most distant point. Nor does a similar movement of skeletal structure always involve the same muscles in tension orientation.

Code is parallel to that used for shoulder, arm, etc., and follows same logic. Instead of # signal which indicates a given arm, etc., ʎ is used to indicate leg. R ʎ ħ symbolizes right leg. ʎʎ indicates both legs.

ʎ 01   Hip-upper leg joint.

ʎ 12   Upper leg-lower leg (knee) joint.

ʎ 23   Lower leg-foot joint (ankle).

Tension is indicated by X under leg section number. Thus ʎ 2 indicates tensed calf.
X

Angle formation indicated in same way as for arm. Thus ʎ⁽ᵐ⁾ʎ 01(6)12(6) 23(3) would be the formula for standing upright, legs together.

Recorder may use the devices shown in the examples above for the arms in his recording of leg activity. However, simpler codes have been devised for certain conventional stances.

Seated

Close double L. Seated, feet square on floor, 01, 12, 23 all at right angles.

Veed L. Legs apart (angle noted from clock) 01, 12, 23 all at right angles.

Close extended. Legs extended 01, 12, 23 angles recorded. Note: legs rest on heels.

Veed extended. Legs extended, 01, 12, 23 angle recorded. Note: legs rest on heels and interleg angle indicated by clock number in leg symbol.

Leg box. Balls of feet touching, legs semi-extended.

Short X. Both feet touching floor, crossed less than half of length from knee to ankle.

Long X. Both feet touching floor, crossed more than half of length from knee to ankle.

Reverse X. Lower legs crossed, feet posterior to knee point.

* Recording of angle probably arbitrary for most patterns.

** Most recorders soon abandon either the λ or the # symbols as they become more proficient with pictographs.

64.

人ᵧ   Tight 4: Legs crossed: total femoral
       contact, knee behind knee.

人Ч   Loose 4: Legs crossed: ankle or foot
       rests on opposing lower extremity of
       femur.

卆†   Over 4: Kneecap over kneecap.

人S   Furled umbrella: Total femoral con-
       tact, total lateral lower leg contact.

人 8   Leg wind: Leg crosses over and then
       foot hooks behind opposing ankle.

人   Tailor: Ankles cross, legs akimbo,
 T   feet under upper thighs or hip.

メ   Up and over: Legs crossed, lateral
人   aspect of both feet rest on superior
       aspect of opposing thighs.

人o   Body ball: Legs together, posterior
       portion of upper legs in total contact
       posterior portion lower legs. Heels
       may contact hip base. *

ๆ   Half-body ball: Same as above except
       only one leg is pulled up.*

人 ⋎⋎ Spread double Vee: Legs spread, pos-
       terior portions of upper and lower legs
       touching. Note angle. Note contact
       point. If hips make contact with sup-
       porting surface note with ⌢ .

* Involvement of arms may be indicated by # sign (s) following
figure.

Seated

Leg dangling or swinging can be recorded by indicating type of 4 plus direction plus member number plus stressed member.

$$\text{4H} \quad \uparrow\downarrow \quad R2 \text{ or } 7 \text{\scriptsize(dotted)} \quad \tfrac{2}{x}$$

Leg joggling is indicated by stutter sign following leg symbol.

$$\lambda R \cdots$$

Foot waving is indicated by direction symbol. In all three of these the usual stress signals may be used.

$$\lambda \ R3 \ \leftrightarrow$$

Summarizing diagrams for arms and legs.

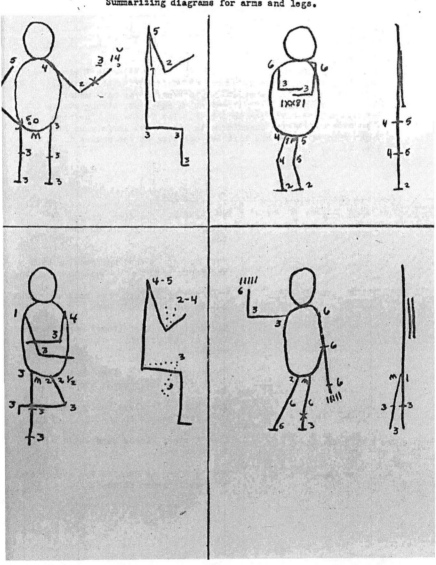

7. Foot behavior.

Standing

To indicate standing, feet symbols are added to leg
pictograph. Short and Long X symbols follow sitting logic.
Angle of Vee indicated by number between legs of pictograph.
Emphasis on one foot indicated by strong stress mark under
foot of pictograph. If all weight on one foot, strong stress
the foot and weak stress the other. The following kinegraph
illustrates a person standing with his weight largely on his
right foot and with his left leg crossing at the ankles in a
long X.

Standing (Feet in motion but not walking)

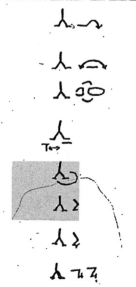

Toe teeter: Standing, rising on
toes, and dropping back on heel and
toe.

Full teeter: Standing, rocking back
and forth from toe to heel to toe, etc.

Foot shuffle: Feet move back and forth
but do not move body away.

Toe dig: One foot (toes) scratch surface of support while other supports
weight.

Standing walk: One leg remains in
place while other moves around it.

Knee bend: Involves bending of knees
with feet square on ground.

Knee teeter: Knees bend while weight
rests on toes.

Stoop: Same as Doubled Vee except that
contact is shown at toes.

Walking

No recording system of manners of walking has been included with this kinegraphic series. Several devices for a
shorthand have been tested and thus far all have proved too
clumsy for either recording or teaching. However, several
general hints may be suggested to steer the observation of
walking styles.

Taking first the male walker (or low heeled shoe walker)
several categories can be described. First the short chi and
the long chi walker. The long chi (X) walker, when taking
a stride involves a swing of the body accentuating the shoulder complementary to the leg moving forward. The short chi
(X) walker swings from the hip without involving the trunk
to a perceptible extent. The long chi walker when adding a
slight lateral swing to the movement of the leg and a slight
lift to the shoulders as part of the anterio-posterior swing
of them may be described as "swaggering" (X).

Generally speaking, when the chi type has been established,
further clarification is provided by the observation of the contact activity of the feet. First, we have the over-kick in
which the leg is swung forward at an angle and a velocity that
the foot swings at the end of the forward motion of the foot
pendulum. Normally, such walkers strike the ground with the
posterior-inferior aspect of the heel when making contact with
the contact surface. This same process may be seen in the
back-kick in which there occurs a sharp posterior bend to the
ankle at the completion of the foot's contact with the contact surface.

The back-kick is probably related to the force of the
push. It has been noted that most walkers may be rated along
a plane from pulling to pushing, some walkers grasping the
ground before them and pulling it to them while others appear to utilize a push action which shoves the body ahead.
At a central point may be placed the balance walker, whose
walk is characterized by the fact that before one set of toes
releases a firm grasp of the ground, the other heel is already
solidly in contact. These three categories, the pusher, the
puller, and the balancer, have provided excellent diagnostic
psychological insights which will be discussed in another
place.

Further classification is provided by the bent knee walker as contrasted with the straight knee walker. Straight and bent knee referring to that period during which the foot is in contact with the contact surface with the body balanced directly above the legs. (There seems to be some correlation between the habitual walking on rough ground and the bent knee walk.)

This leads directly to the categories of bouncers and gliders. These types represent poles. The bouncer generally raises his entire body by rising on his toes as his foot passes directly below the body plane, thus his shoulders can be seen to rise and fall with each step. The glider, coordinates the contact, the ankle bend, and the knee bend so that the body moves forward with the shoulders remaining in the same plane.

Further classes are provided by the high stepper and the foot dragger. The high stepper raises his foot in its swing above the ankle bone of the contact foot. The foot dragger allows the completed foot to drag as it begins its forward swing. The foot dragger is not to be confused with the shuffler who maintains contact with the contact surface with both feet throughout walk, or the foot stutterer, who allows the toes to drag in a staccato manner at the end of the contact.

The length of the stride provides one other dimension to the consideration of walking styles. Generally speaking, the earlier classifications are more important in the description of the walker than is length of stride. However, two types stand out. The dipper lengthens his stride to the point that his body is lowered at the end point of each stride. This may be a variation on the glide inasmuch as the length of the stride involves maintaining contact to avoid falling. The choppy walker may be a variation on the high stepper. The difference between the two is that the choppy walker seldom extends the forward moving foot more than a single foot length beyond the contact foot.

Since balance is maintained usually by the use of the arms, these are to be correlated with the types discussed above. There are a number of arm classes which have already been isolated. The stiff arm moves his arms from the shoulders and allows little break at the joints. This tends to give a staccato appearance to the walk and should be examined apart from the leg motion. The lower arm mover tends to keep the upper arm within the trunk plane while swinging the lower arm. Balance difficulties again give the appearance of an uncertain gait. The chugger should be mentioned. This concerns the arms held with #(12) at 3o'clock (generally the hands are in fist). The double swing in which both arms move in parallel fashion is uncommon among Americans but does appear in the Far East.

As observed American middle majority walkers seem to move
the arm to about five o'clock at each step, the length of the
arm swing increasing with the pace until about four o'clock may
be reached by some walkers. Only two walkers have been observed
to reach a three o'clock swing and both of these were ex-members
of the Canadian Army.

The movements of the body and the head add final variables
to our discussion. Several of these deserve attention. Again
it must be stressed that if the observer will abstract the various parts, leg, arm, and body and then combine them he is likely
to avoid certain ethnocentric or egocentric impressions. As
stances, five types have been isolated. The first of these is
the slump in which the shoulders are lowered and/or rolled anteriorly or medially. The reverse of this is the rared back in
which the shoulders are pulled posteriorly. Two others which
may be distinguished are the ramrod and the military. Although
both of these are characterized by the "squareness" of the
shoulders, the ramrod involves more tension in the pectoral and
upper arm musculature. The sidle is characterized by the fact
fact that one shoulder is consistently more anteriorly advanced
than the other. This may involve a full trunk twist or posterior-
anterior placement of the shoulders.

Three other variations on trunk activity may be noted full
trunk projection, in which the body is held nearly perpendicular,
the legs make little anterior stretch, and the feet seem to make
extended contact with the contact surface behind the body plane;
the abdominal projection, whether a resultant of hyper-lordosis,
the size of the abdominal region, or a combination of either of
these with the rare-back, projects the medial area of the body
anteriorly; the pelvic projection, in which the pelvic region is
thrust forward, the curvature usually beginning in the lombar
region and culminating at the sacro-illiac.

> The terminology utilized in this section is evi-
> dently ethnocentric; it is hoped that the descrip-
> tions are sufficiently non-normative to overcome
> this. The terms employed were chosen because they
> are meaningful to most speakers of English and ex-
> pedite learning and memory.

There is less difference between male and female walking than
is popularly supposed except that there is a differential selection from among the types. Most of the same categories apply to
both male and female walkers. However, the wearing of "high heels"
or "platform" shoes do greatly effect the general appearance of

the walk. Observers are warned to record together with the
physical description a statement concerning the type of foot-
wear and the type of skirt worn. Both exert considerable influence over the walk, the stance, and the gait. Too, the
breast development may give a delusory aspect to the entire
walk. Only by the careful segmental analysis can this be
avoided.

While flat-footed walkers occur among both males and females, shoe types probably lead to a higher incidence among
females. In this the whole foot is placed down at once. Of
these there are two evident types. The trudger who places
his feet down flat footed and who combines flat-footedness with
pulling. A second type, less common among males, is the toe-
point flat foot in which at each step the foot is placed down
squarely but the toe is always pointed in a direct anterior
line. This is seldom seen with a fast gait.

Pidgeon-toeing, in which the toes point medio-anterior-
ally at each step, the duck walk in which the toes point latero-
anteriorally, the so-called Indian walk in which the feet are
placed directly in front of each other at each step are common
enough to be noted.

All of this section should be carefully analyzed
against material taken from observations of other
cultures. Caution is needed in making descriptions. Note that the Arab describes a woman who
walks "gracefully" as "walking like a chicken."
The Indian describes a "graceful" woman as "walking
like an elephant." The should deter those who
wish to avoid physically descriptive statements.

8. <u>The neck.</u>

Anterior projection

Posterior projection

Right lateral projection

Left lateral projection

Neck tense

Neck sag

Swallowing

Adams Apple Jump

Neck Twist Right

Neck Twist Left

SUGGESTED READINGS

Bateson, Gregory and Mead, Margaret. Balinese Character. A Photographic Analysis. New York, The New York Academy of Sciences, 1942.

Brewer, W. D. Patterns of Gesture among the Levantine Arabs. American Anthropologist, Vol. 53, No. 2, 1951.

Cochiara, G. Il linguaggio del gesto. Turin, Bocca, 1932.

Craighead, Jean C. A System of Notation for the Modern Dance. Philadelphia, 1942 (typewritten).

Critchley, M. The Language of Gesture. London and New York, Edward Arnold, Longmans Green, 1939.

Dunlap, K. A Project for Investigating the Facial Signs of Personality. American Journal of Psychology, 39, 156-161, 1927.

Efron, D. Gesture and Environment. New York, Kings Crown Press, 1941.

———— and Foley, J. P., Jr. Gestural Behavior and Social Setting. Zeitschrift f. Sozialforsch., 6, 152-161, 1937.

Flachkampf, L. Spanische Gebärdensprache, Roman Forschung. 52, 205-208, 1938.

Gesell, Arnold L. Studies in Child Development. New York, Harper, 1948.

Giese, F. Psychologie der Arbeithand. Berlin-Wien, Urban and Schwartzenburg, 1928.

Huber, E. Evolution of Facial Musculature and Facial Expression. Baltimore, Johns Hopkins Press, 1931.

Hughes, Russell Merriwether, (La Meri) The Gesture Language of the Hindu Dance, New York, Columbia University Press, 1941.

James, W. T. A Study of the Expression of Bodily Posture. Journal of Genetic Psychology 7, 405-437, 1932.

Krout, M. H. Autistic Gestures, An Experimental Study in Symbolic Movement, Psychological Monograph 46, No. 208, 1935.

———— A Preliminary Note on some Obscure Symbolic Muscular Responses of Diagnostic Value in the Study of Normal Subjects. American Journal of Psychology, 11, 29-71, 1931.

———— The Social and Psychological Significance of Gestures (A Differential Analysis). Journal of Genetic Psychology. 47, 385-412, 1935.

———— Symbolic Gestures in the Clinical Study of Personality. Trans. Illinois State Academy of Science, 24, 519-523, 1931.

Klineberg, Otto Racial Differences in Speed and Accuracy. Journal of Abnormal and Social Psychology. 22, 273-277, 1927.

Labarre, Weston. The Cultural Basis of Emotions and Gestures. Journal of Personality, 16, 49-68, 1947.

Lersch, P. Die Bedeutung des Mimischen Ausdruckserscheinungen fur die Beurteilung der Personlichkeit, Indus Psychotechn, 5, 178-183, 1928.

———— Gesicht und Seele. Grundlinien einer mimischen Diagnostik, Dresden, Reinhardt, 1932.

Lifer, Serge. Annotation of Movement, Kinetography (in Russian) Art Publishing House, Moscow, 1940.

Lynn, J. G. and Lynn, D. R. Smile and Hand Dominance in Relation to Basic Modes of Adaptation, Journal of Abnormal and Social Psychology, 38, 250-276, 1943.

Maranon, Gregario The Psychology of Gesture, Journal of Nervous and Mental Diseases, 112, 469-497, 1950.

Masson-Oursel, P. Le rôle des attitudes dans la conception indienne de la vie, Psychologie et Vie, 4, 23-24, 1930.

Mead, Margaret and MacGregor, Frances. Growth and Culture, New York, Putnam, 1951.

Minkowski, M. Sur les mouvements, les réflexes, les réactions musculaires du foetus humain de 2 à 5 mois et leur relations avec le système nerveux foetal, Rev. Neur, 37, 1105-1135, 1921.

Murphy, Gardiner Personality, New York, Harpers, 1947.

Ombredane, A. Études de pschologie medicale. II Geste et action, Rio de Janeiro, Atlantica Editora, 1944.

Paget, R. A. S. Gesture Language, Nature, London, 39, 1937.

Pandeya, Gayanacharya A. The Art of Kathakali. Kitabistan, Allabahabad, 1943.

Pengniez, P. Cinématique de la main; la main du prestidigatateur. Presse Medicale, 35, 123-125, 1927.

Pollenz, Phillippa Methods for the Comparative Study of the Dance, American Anthropologist, New Series, Vol. 51, No. 3, 428-435, 1949.

Rosa, L. A. Espressioni e mimica. Milan, Hoepli, 1929.

Schilder, P. The Image and Appearance of the Human Body. New York, International Universities Press, 1950.

Schlauch, M. Recent Soviet Studies in Linguistics. Science and Society, New York, 1, 152-167, 1936.

Schuhl, Pierre-Maxime Remarque sur le regard, Journal de Psychologie Normale et Pathologique 41, 184-193, 1948.

Strehle, H. Analyse des Gebardens. Indus. Psychotechn., 11, 89-90, 1934.

————— Analyse des Gebardens. Erforschung des Ausdrucks der Korpesbewegung. Berlin, Bernard u. Graefe, 1935.

Venkatachalam, G. Dance in India. Bombay, Nalanda Publications, 194?.

Weiss, P. The Social Character of Gestures, Philosophical Review, 52, 182-186, 1943.

Wenger, M. A. An Attempt to Appraise Individual Differences in Level of Muscular Tension. Journal of Experimental Psychology, 32, 213-225, 1943.

Witte, O. Untersuchen uber die Gebardensprache. Beitrage zur Psychologie der Sprache. Zeitschrift fur Psychologie, 116, 225-308, 1930.

Wolff, Werner The Expression of Personality: Experimental Depth Psychology, 1943.

Addendum *

From Seminar, May 27, 1952
R. Birdwhistell, Chas. A. Fer
H. Smith, and G. Trager.
Revision of Page 22.

Prekinesics:

  Somatic shifts
  Abstracted somatic shifts: Kine

Prelinguistics:

  Phone

Microkinesics:

Kinology
    Kinics: Kine as allokine
      1. Stress,
        Completion.
      2. Structural
        variation.
    Kinemics: Kineme

Microlinguistics:

Phonology
    Phonetics: Phone a
           allophc
    Phonemics: Phoneme

Kinemorphemics:
1. Kinemorpheme: Systematic recur-
   rence of one or more kinemes, the
   whole having differential meaning.
   (Kinemorph: a single instance, an
   allokinomorph of a kinemorpheme).

2. Kinemorphemic construction:
   a combination of kinemorphemes.

Morphemics:
1. Morphophonemics: Morphs as
   allomorphs of morpheme.

2. Arrangement
   A. Morphology (words).

   B. Syntax (constructions)
      a. phrases
      b. clauses
      c. sentences

Social Kinesics:

1. Act: One or more kinemorphemes in
   context in one body area.

2. Action: A combination of acts.

3. Scene: Combination of actions.

Metalinguistics:

1. Phonology
   Morphology
   Syntax

2. Utterance (Sentence in conte:

3. Discourse

---

* See page following for kinesic examples of various levels.

Discussion of Addendum Chart

The chart above was derived from seminar discussion after the manuscript had gone to press. As can be seen, it draws a closer parallel between the methodologies utilized in the study of communication devices.

Using the "wink" example cited above we can illustrate the kinesics aspects of the outline. On the pre-kinesic level the wink is a neuro-muscular occurrence which may involve facial, head, neck and various other body musculature and skeletal parts. The kine is the smallest abstractable unit of aspects of any of the parts, that is, the least unit of body motion with discrimination-al meaning.

Turning to microkinesic analysis, experiment reveals that the various kines may be variedly produced in structural organization or in degree of stress or extent of completion of the particular motion. These variations, which do not change differential meaning, are described as allokinic. From the abstraction of the class of allokines is derived the given kineme which may be lid closure, or head set, or brow position, or mouth behavior, etc.

Each of the test examples given in the text of the wink is a kinemorph. A kinemorpheme is an abstraction, being a class of kinemorphs which have been experimentally derived. Thus, a given situation in which one person closes the lid in a given way with the face, head, etc. in given positions or motions, is a kinemorph. The general class of behavior which is abstractable as "wink" is a kinemorpheme. A combination of kinemorphemes (with differential meaning) is a kinemorphemic construction.

In context we are concerned with the "wink" in a social situation and which is identified as being an aspect of a social behavioral series and in which meaning is defined in terms of the role played by the presence or absence of the given act or action in the communication situation. Act is defined as one or more kinemorphemes in context as abstracted from one body area. Action is the description of a combination of acts. Act and action are discriminated as a precautionary device against the easy assumption that the behavior observed in one body area is all the behavior that is taking place at a given time.

The term scene is used to describe the total kinesic recording during a given (time duration and space-defined field) communication situation. The "wink" would thus represent one aspect of the total kinesic-linguistic recording which takes place in the description of social meaning (communication as measured by behavioral shifts).

DATE DUE
DATE DE RETOUR

DEC 0 8 2001	
DEC 0 3 2001	
FEB 2 7 2002	
FEB 2 5 2002	

7

Printed in the USA
CPSIA information can be obtained
at www.ICGtesting.com
LVHW020427280124
770073LV00001B/165